BLACK ZEN

BEGINNER'S GUIDE TO MEDITATION

by

Jasmine Johnson

and

Stacey Johnson

© 2018 Jasmine Johnson and Stacey Johnson

All rights reserved. No part of this book may be reproduced in any form or by any information storage and retrieval system or technologies now known or later developed, without the permission in writing from the publisher.

For information about this publication or other written work from the authors, email info@blackzen.co.

ISBN 978-0-692-15357-4

Published by Black Zen

Blackzen.co

Graphic Design: *Veronika Grebennikova*
Copy Edit: *Kimberly Brummell*

CONTENTS

V	Preface
01	First Things First
04	Sit Down & Shut Up
05	Ways To Find Quiet
09	Master Consistency
10	Common FAQ
11	Real Talk
13	Help Along The Way
15	Practice Guide
16	Progress Tracker
17	Journal & Workbook

PREFACE

This guide is dedicated to those who are seeking to change the trajectory of their life, looking for a way to do things differently, and most of all, to those who are curious about the best way to create positive change.

In the beginning of the guide, we've provided the basics to begin a meditation practice and answered common questions that may arise when starting out. Following this set of instructions is a 6-week customizable practice guide that will help you stay consistent and grow deeper in your meditation practice.

To get the most out of this guide, we recommend journaling about your experiences on a regular basis and reflecting on the prompts located within the lined pages.

Above all else, be patient with yourself and your progress. Developing a meditation practice is a great tool to helping you reach your next level. Let's get started!

ELEVATE

WELCOME TO THE BLACK ZEN BEGINNER'S GUIDE TO MEDITATION

BLACK ZEN is a social enterprise dedicated to making meditation accessible, relatable, and effective across a dynamic range of people. In this guide, we aim to provide a brief introduction to meditation, along with encouragement and quick tips to help you start a consistent meditation practice. We believe that with a clear mind you'll be able to move forward faster, find joy, and take pleasure in the process to getting there.

It is never too late
to turn on the light...

When you flip the switch in that attic,
it doesn't matter whether its been dark
for ten minutes, ten years
or ten decades.

The light still illuminates the room
and banishes the murkiness,
letting you see the things
you couldn't see before.

- Sharon Salzberg

WHAT

■ SO WHAT IS MEDITATION?

Meditation is an intentional exercise to quiet the mind and increase internal awareness. Internal awareness is our ability to recognize the parts of us below the surface that shape our thoughts and dictate our behavior.

■ IS THAT THE SAME THING AS MINDFULNESS?

While meditation and mindfulness both promote developing a higher level of awareness, the targets of this increased awareness differ. While mindfulness aims to increase our awareness of outer experiences, meditation shifts our attention towards inward reflection.

WHO

■ WHO CAN BE A MEDITATOR?

Despite commonly held beliefs, meditation is not restricted to monks, Buddhists, or even the religious. Just as the practice of sitting in silence is open to anyone and everyone, so are the benefits that meditation offers. You don't have to travel to Tibet to find your zen. Just keep reading…

Sit Down

Shut up

FIRST

▪ HOW DO YOU BEGIN?

The truth is, sitting down and quieting the mind is not as simple as it sounds. For those that have tried it, you know the mind is constantly racing with thoughts ranging from the mundane to the profound. Yet most of those thoughts are either worrying about the past (e.g. Did I make the right decision? Why did that happen to me?) or wondering about the future (e.g. What's my next move?).

The goal of meditation is to bring your thoughts into the present moment. Start by removing distractions.

- Find a quiet location and turn that phone on silent. We know this is hard, but it's important to maintaining concentration.
- Sit in a comfortable seated position, either with legs crossed on the floor, or feet planted on the ground in a highbacked chair.
- Take as much time as you need to get settled. If you sit and realize you're thirsty, quickly grab water. If you're chilly, grab a sweater.

The more of these little things you can take care of in the beginning, the better. Your mind will have run through the mental checklist of small comforts to hopefully silence itself of physical needs. Once these have been attended to, then the mind typically shifts to EVERYTHING else! It's this everything else that meditation aims to silence.

▪ WAYS TO QUIET YOUR MIND

Now that you're physically ready, it's time to start the meditation. We're all unique and everyone has a different way of finding silence. We've provided three options to help give you an idea of where to begin.

▪ USE YOUR BREATH

Begin listening and paying close attention to your inhale and exhale. With eyes closed, carefully follow each breath as it creates sensations throughout your body.

Start to notice how it feels when inhaling and exhaling through your nose. Next, turn your attention to your chest as it rises and falls with each breath. Lastly, notice how your stomach moves in and out in time with your breathing.

Paying attention to each of these areas (nose, chest, or stomach) can naturally create an inner stillness. What makes this method so effective is that the breath is always available, so it can become a great focal point in your practice.

GIVE YOUR MIND
a Focal Point

Since thoughts are consistently generating, giving your mind a simple task can help you stay more focused in your meditation practice. The goal of using a focal point is to keep your attention on a specific point of reference.

Using this technique provides a focal point you can return to when you find yourself distracted or when your thoughts begin to wander.

We've found focusing on the tip of your nose helpful if you prefer to sit with your eyes closed. With eyes open, you can use simple objects like a stone or even a flame to hold your attention.

Try experimenting with different focal points to find which option works best for you, but make sure the object you choose is something fairly simple so it can provide a plain slate for you to observe.

LET GO

■ THE BUBBLE TECHNIQUE

If you find it difficult to focus on your breath or your chosen focal point, you can also try what we playfully refer to as the bubble technique. Imagine all of your incoming thoughts as bubbles floating by in your mind.

Don't try to dissect or study them, simply watch them as they pass. Observe them without judgement or comment. Over time, you'll begin to notice less "bubbles" and your mind will gradually quiet down.

ACTION

■ **NOW THAT YOU HAVE A FEW METHODS TO TRY, IT'S TIME TO PUT THEM INTO ACTION**

- Find a comfortable and quiet place to practice, and choose 1 of the techniques.
- Set your phone timer for 1–2 minutes (If you're feeling cocky crank it up to 5, but remember, it's better to find quiet for 30 seconds than it is to sit with a racing mind for 5).
- Start the clock and go!

Congratulations!
You've just started your meditation practice

NEXT

First time experiences will vary, as will the duration of stillness found within that 1–5 minutes. Consider 10-30 seconds of focus or silence a win.

If you found 10–30 seconds impossible, hang in there. We promise it gets easier!

A BIG TIP
On How To Stay Consistent

Create a physical space for your meditation that feels special and make it an area that you're excited to come to each day. An enjoyable place lends itself to an enjoyable experience, and an enjoyable experience will be one that you will happily repeat!

It also helps to find a consistent time in your day that you can devote to silence. Setting aside 2–3 minutes at the same time on a regular basis will help build your meditation practice as a habit. Just a few minutes each day can make a significant difference in your mood and your mindset, even when you're not actively meditating.

FAQ

■ FREQUENTLY ASKED QUESTIONS

After the first (or 100th!) meditation session, many have questions. Here are a few...

AM I DOING THIS RIGHT?

The good news is, there is no such thing as doing it "right". The only measure of success is your consistency with the practice. Like a muscle, you can't do 10 squats for one day and expect to see results. Keep working at it over time, and slowly but surely, you'll begin to see changes.

FOR HOW LONG SHOULD I MEDITATE?

We recommend starting with 1–2 minutes a day. When that feels easy, try increasing to 2 minutes in the morning as soon as you wake-up and 2 minutes at night before going to bed. Over time, this duration will increase, but remember:

Consistency over duration is the key to seeing results!

■ THE TOUGH QUESTIONS

Now for the REAL.

Here are the questions you may have but might be too timid to ask...

WON'T I LOOK CRAZY JUST SITTING HERE IN SILENCE?

Crazy is doing the same thing over and over again and expecting a different result. When you are ready to grow, the real question is are you crazy to not try something that's been proven to enhance your quality of life?

HOW CAN MEDITATION HELP WITH REAL ISSUES LIKE BILLS AND LIFE?!

Meditation brings clarity and focus to any situation. These two elements combined will help you uncover what you need to overcome challenges, both personal and financial. Not to mention, the peace that a meditation practice provides allows for a life that is much more enjoyable in the meantime.

IS THE JUICE WORTH THE SQUEEZE?

Absolutely! Spending time on building a meditation practice may not be the easiest thing to do, but the benefits are nothing less than incredible.

When you're ambitious but perpetually feeling stuck, nothing will get you moving forward faster than a consistent meditation practice.

CAN MEDITATION HELP ME BECOME MORE CALM AND LESS ANXIOUS?

Yes. Meditation slows down your thoughts and reactions so that you can approach drama from a cool and collected place. This leads to a more calculated, better approach to facing adversity.

CAN MEDITATING HELP WITH PHYSICAL PAIN?

It is said that pain begins in the mind. There is a small portion of time that occurs between a stimulus (e.g. pain) and our reaction to it (e.g. thoughts about the pain that only deepen our awareness of how much it hurts). Relax the mind, relax the muscles. Does this mean toss the aspirin? No. We're saying meditation can change our relationship to pain, and thus, lessen its impact on us throughout the day.

PRACTICAL TIPS
to Help You Move Through the 6-Week Guide

1
START WHERE YOU ARE

It's important to not compare your process with others', or evaluate yourself as you're meditating. We all want to get the proverbial "A" when we set out to do something new, but the truth is, developing a practice will be based on multiple factors (e.g. where you are in your life, what you've been exposed to, etc.).

2
PAY ATTENTION TO POSTURE

Whether you're cross-legged on the floor or sitting in a chair, be sure to keep your back straight. This helps with your breathing and keeps your body alert during your meditation.

3
THINK OF MEDITATION AS A PRACTICE

There will be stops and starts along the way, and some days your practice may be deeper than others. Like all things, you'll get better the more you practice and your ability to re-center and find silence will improve over time.

PRACTICE

■ **GETTING STARTED WITH YOUR 6-WEEK PRACTICE**

As a beginning meditator, sometimes the hardest thing to do is maintain consistency. In the following pages, you'll find a customizable 6-week calendar that provides an easy way to track your progress, tools to develop a system that works best for you, and practice suggestions that will help you stay on track.

See if you notice a difference between meditating first thing in the morning versus just before bed. Notice if you find it easier to quiet your mind after a few moments or if it feels better having longer meditations that allow you to ease into quiet. Use the next 6 weeks to explore what feels right for you.

Lastly, we've added pages for notes to record insights, more tips to help you on your journey, and helpful prompts to connect what you're experiencing "on the mat" with how that might show up in your daily life. We're happy to be your partners in progress and excited for you to get started!

WEEK 1 | FINDING CALM AND STILLNESS

Describe each day's experience or the technique practiced.

SUNDAY _____
Location: _____

Time: _____ am/pm

MONDAY _____
Location: _____

Time: _____ am/pm

TUESDAY _____
Location: _____

Time: _____ am/pm

WEDNESDAY _____
Location: _____

Time: _____ am/pm

THURSDAY _____
Location: _____

Time: _____ am/pm

FRIDAY _____
Location: _____

Time: _____ am/pm

SATURDAY _____
Location: _____

Time: _____ am/pm

UTILIZING DIFFERENT TECHNIQUES

Use the instructions on pages 5–8 to begin practicing each meditation technique. Give each method a try for a few days before moving on to the next. Doing this will help you find what works best for you. Once you know, you can start customizing a practice that is easier and more enjoyable to maintain.

As you begin to quiet your mind, you may be surprised at what comes up during your meditations. Without judgement, just begin to observe where your thoughts lead and rather than creating a story around them, keep gently bringing yourself back to your focal point. After your meditation, use these pages to note your observations.

WEEK 2 | CONSISTENCY IS KEY

Describe each day's experience or the technique practiced.

SUNDAY
Location: _____

Time: _____ am/pm

MONDAY
Location: _____

Time: _____ am/pm

TUESDAY
Location: _____

Time: _____ am/pm

WEDNESDAY
Location: _____

Time: _____ am/pm

THURSDAY
Location: _____

Time: _____ am/pm

FRIDAY
Location: _____

Time: _____ am/pm

SATURDAY
Location: _____

Time: _____ am/pm

SETTING A SPECIFIC TIME TO PRACTICE

In addition to the tips on page 9, one of the best ways to build a habit is to make it easy to do. Setting your meditation time before or after something you always do each day helps to provide an easy, intuitive, and consistent reminder to practice.

Rather than focusing on the duration of time you're able to sit, remember that consistency is the key to a strong practice. Mastering the discipline of showing up to meditate every day is the best measure of progress.

WEEK 3 | WORKING WITH YOUR ENVIRONMENT

Describe each day's experience or the technique practiced.

SUNDAY _____
Location: _____

Time: _____ am/pm

MONDAY _____
Location: _____

Time: _____ am/pm

TUESDAY _____
Location: _____

Time: _____ am/pm

WEDNESDAY _____
Location: _____

Time: _____ am/pm

THURSDAY _____
Location: _____

Time: _____ am/pm

FRIDAY _____
Location: _____

Time: _____ am/pm

SATURDAY _____
Location: _____

Time: _____ am/pm

USING SOUND TO YOUR ADVANTAGE

In week 1, you began experimenting with different areas of focus such as observing your breath or acknowledging thoughts as they came up without attaching any judgements or stories to them. This week, see if you can apply the same principles to the sounds in your environment. Some examples could be having a soft focus on the sound of a ceiling fan, listening to the rush of cars outside, or even just maintaining an awareness of the white noise in your room.

In the same way that we're encouraging you to use the unconventional method of using sound in your environment as an anchor rather than a distraction, as your awareness grows, you may notice that there are many ways to approach difficult or frustrating moments that occur in day-to-day life. Open up to the idea of using unconventional avenues in overcoming these obstacles as well.

WEEK 4 | BROADEN YOUR AWARENESS

Describe each day's experience or the technique practiced.

SUNDAY
Location: _____

Time: _____ am/pm

MONDAY
Location: _____

Time: _____ am/pm

TUESDAY
Location: _____

Time: _____ am/pm

WEDNESDAY
Location: _____

Time: _____ am/pm

THURSDAY
Location: _____

Time: _____ am/pm

FRIDAY
Location: _____

Time: _____ am/pm

SATURDAY
Location: _____

Time: _____ am/pm

BECOMING AN ACTIVE OBSERVER

The more we meditate, the more observant we become of our environment. We may begin to notice how external situations affect our inner experience, or become more aware of our own thoughts, behaviors, and quality of our conversations.

On page 11, we mentioned a consistent meditation practice will increase clarity and focus in all aspects of life. Begin to observe your day-to-day activities and use that increased clarity and focus to notice how certain situations and/or people make you feel. Use these findings to adjust your environment, company, and behavior if needed.

WEEK 5 | DEEPEN YOUR PRACTICE

Describe each day's experience or the technique practiced.

SUNDAY _____
Location: _____

Time: _____ am/pm

MONDAY _____
Location: _____

Time: _____ am/pm

TUESDAY _____
Location: _____

Time: _____ am/pm

WEDNESDAY _____
Location: _____

Time: _____ am/pm

THURSDAY _____
Location: _____

Time: _____ am/pm

FRIDAY _____
Location: _____

Time: _____ am/pm

SATURDAY _____
Location: _____

Time: _____ am/pm

DEVOTING TIME TO YOUR PRACTICE

When we value something, we put our time and attention into it. Your meditation practice is no different. If you've already found consistency, try extending your sit by a few minutes. Extending the amount of time you sit in meditation can be a great way to deepen your concentration and find more sustained periods of inner stillness.

Often when we begin quieting the mind, certain areas of our life that need our attention will start to reveal themselves. Now is a great time to look back through your notes and see if there are certain themes that consistently arise after your meditation.

WEEK 6 | MAINTAIN YOUR PEACE

Describe each day's experience or the technique practiced.

SUNDAY
Location: _____

Time: _____ am/pm

MONDAY
Location: _____

Time: _____ am/pm

TUESDAY
Location: _____

Time: _____ am/pm

WEDNESDAY
Location: _____

Time: _____ am/pm

THURSDAY
Location: _____

Time: _____ am/pm

FRIDAY
Location: _____

Time: _____ am/pm

SATURDAY
Location: _____

Time: _____ am/pm

HAVING PATIENCE WITH YOUR PROGRESS

You did it! You made it through the first 6 weeks of your meditation practice. This is a huge accomplishment and you should be proud of yourself. Go back and review your notes from week 1 for extra encouragement to see just how far you've come.

You're at the end of this workbook, but your journey doesn't stop here. Now that you've experimented with different techniques to determine the style, time of day, and location that works best for you, set up your own tracking process for the next 6 weeks or even 6 months. Sticking to a daily practice will have huge benefits over time. Results may not always be immediate, but with a consistent practice, they are inevitable.

FIND YOUR PATH

At BLACK ZEN we treat meditation as a basic thing you do each day to maintain a healthy and clear mind. We think of meditation as part of a daily routine like brushing your teeth or washing your face each morning. You wouldn't leave your house without doing those things, and similarly, you shouldn't start your day without first centering yourself.

There is a way to live a life that is peaceful and at ease, while still thoughtfully moving forward to reach your goals. Meditation is a tool to help you get there. It is our hope that this beginner's guide sparked some interest, gave useful tips, and cleared up common misconceptions as you start your own practice. But remember, information is only useful if you apply it!

ABOUT THE AUTHORS

Black Zen's founders share over 15 years of meditation experience and study (both formal and informal), and draw from these collective insights, lessons, and experiences when sharing and curating content. The approach to meditation is nonreligious in nature and focuses only on the practice of sitting and intentionally quieting the mind for personal growth.

BLACK ZEN was specifically created to remove the social and financial barriers that restrict black and brown communities from discovering the benefits of meditation, and to allow a space for every community to feel included in wellness-based practices.

Photo: *Russ Quackenbush*

www.ingramcontent.com/pod-product-compliance
Lightning Source LLC
Chambersburg PA
CBRC092342290426
44110CB00008B/184